MAR 3 1 1998

A WORLD OF HOLIDAYS

Passover

A WORLD OF HOLIDAYS

Passover

David Rose
and
Gill Rose

RSVP
**RAINTREE
STECK-VAUGHN**
P U B L I S H E R S
The Steck-Vaughn Company

Austin, Texas

Published by Raintree Steck-Vaughn Publishers, an imprint of Steck-Vaughn Company

Library of Congress Cataloging-in-Publication Data

Rose, David W.
    Passover / David Rose and Gill Rose.
      p.   cm. — (A world of holidays)
    Includes bibliographical references and index.
   Summary: Introduces the traditions and customs associated with the celebration of Passover and with the seder meal.
    ISBN 0-8172-4607-X
    1. Passover—Juvenile literature.   2. Seder—Juvenile literature.
[1. Passover. 2. Seder] I. Rose, Gill (Gill D.), 1949–
II. Title.   III. Series.
BM695.P3R66   1997
296.4'37—dc20   96-42306
                                    CIP
                                      AC

Printed in Spain
Bound in the United States
1 2 3 4 5 6 7 8 9 0 99 98 97 96

To the Reader:
In the book on Passover, you will discover that there are differences in the practice of religion among Jews. Some of the practices described in this book are usually followed by Orthodox Jews. Jews can also be members of Reform, Conservative, or Reconstructionist groups.

ACKNOWLEDGMENTS

Editors: Su Swallow, Pam Wells
Design: Neil Sayer
Production: Jenny Mulvanny

The author and publishers would like to thank Anne Clark for her help and support in the preparation of this text, and the staff and children of the Independent Jewish Day School, London, for their help and cooperation in the making of some of the images in this book. Thanks are due to Rabbi Lawrence Groffman for reading and advising on the manuscript.

For permission to reproduce copyright material, the authors and publishers gratefully acknowledge the following:

Title page: Trip/H Rogers
Contents page: Trip/H Rogers
page 6 David Rose page 7 (top) David Rose, (bottom) Zefa page 8 Trip/H Rogers page 9 David Rose page 10 (top) Nancy Durrell McKenna/Panos Pictures, (bottom) Robert Harding Picture Library page 11 (top) Liba Taylor/Hutchison Library, (bottom) David Rose page 12 Ancient Art and Architecture Collection, (bottom) Trip/H Rogers page 13 David Rose page 14 (top) Trip/Muzlish, (bottom) David Rose page 15 Ancient Art and Architecture page 16 (top) Trip/P Mitchell, (bottom) Trip/H Rogers page 17 Ancient Art and Architecture page 18 Zefa page 19 (top) David Rose, (bottom) Circa Photo Library/Barrie Searle page 20/21 David Rose page 22 Trip/M Jenkin page 23 (top) Liba Taylor/Hutchison Library, (bottom) David Rose page 24 Michael J O'Brien/Panos Pictures page 25 (left) Ancient Art and Architecture, (right) David Rose page 26 (left) Angela Silvertop/Hutchison Library, (right) Nancy Durrell McKenna/Hutchison Library page 27 David Rose 28/29 Alan Towse Photography

Contents

It's Spring Again

Passover takes place in the spring. It lasts for a week, but the main event is a special meal, called the Seder.

Jerusalem, in Israel, is the center of Judaism, the religion of Jewish people.

LOOKING BACK, AND FORWARD

Passover is a time when Jewish people look back to important events in their history. It is also a time when they look forward to the future, in the hope of better times to come. The holiday, or festival, dates back more than 3,000 years. It reminds Jews of the the time when they were slaves in Egypt, and God freed them from slavery. This event is called the Exodus. It is written about in the book of the Bible called Exodus.

FAMILY FUN

Jews usually share this holiday with their family, and children especially have a lot of fun. Many families invite friends or others to share their Seder if they have nowhere else to go. For some Jewish families everything changes in the home at Passover. The food is different, and even the plates, silverware, and glasses are different from what is used the rest of the year. People greet each other by saying "Hag Sameach," which means "Happy Holiday" in Hebrew.

The center of the Jewish world is Jerusalem, in Israel. Passover, which is also called Pesach, begins when the new moon is seen in Jerusalem, and everyone prepares for the Seder.

▲ Two boys reading Hebrew.

A Jewish family enjoying the Seder.

7

 Spring Cleaning the House

Every year when the time of Passover comes near, Jewish people know they must start to get the house ready from top to bottom.

FORBIDDEN FOODS

Springtime is traditionally a time of spring cleaning. For Jewish people, part of their spring cleaning is to clear out food that is not special for Passover. Jews do not eat foods with leaven during this holiday. Leavened foods contain yeast, so most breads and crackers are banned.

Children join in the search for leavened food, which the Jews call *chametz*. Some people leave a bit of chametz in each room so the children can look for it on the evening before the holiday begins. In some families, the children use a candle to see by, and a feather for brushing up the forbidden crumbs.

A candle and a feather are used to hunt *chametz*.

CHANGES!

Some families put away the everyday pots and pans, plates, and knives and forks. Often, these are placed in a cupboard that is then sealed up for the eight days of the holiday. Special dishes and cutlery are taken out and carefully washed to be ready for Passover.

On the day of the Seder, the table is carefully laid with the special Passover plates, knives, and forks. Candlesticks are polished and flowers arranged. Everyone is looking forward to the evening celebrations.

Children at a Jewish elementary school wash the cutlery to prepare for their Seder.

A table set for the Seder.

Kosher Cooking

All year long, some Jews follow rules about what foods they eat and how they are cooked. At Passover, there are more special rules about their food.

A Jewish family in Israel enjoying an evening meal.

FIT AND PROPER

Food that Jews are allowed to eat is called kosher, which means "fit" or "proper." In the book of Leviticus, in the Bible, there is a list of animals that can be eaten. These animals are kosher. For example, Jews can eat any fish that has scales and fins, but they are not allowed to eat shellfish.

Kosher foods must be cooked in a certain way, too. One rule is that milk and meat must never be mixed together or eaten at the same meal.

Fish like these are kosher.

10

A mother and her daughter prepare a kosher meal.

Shopping for kosher foods.

For example, a hamburger followed by a yogurt would not be allowed. In some Jewish homes, the kitchen has one part for cooking meats and another for cooking milk foods. Life is much easier for vegetarians!

EATING SPECIAL FOODS

At Passover, leavened food—food with yeast—is not allowed. Only unleavened food is kosher for Passover. Many Jews like to shop in stores that have special sections for kosher foods.

Baking Bread and Burning the Chametz

Bread is an important part of most people's diet. At Passover, bread has a special meaning for Jews.

COOKING IN A HURRY

Passover is also called the Feast of Unleavened Bread. This is because only unleavened bread is eaten at this time. Bread without leaven (yeast) does not rise; when it is baked, it stays flat. This kind of bread is called *matzah*. Matzah

 Blessing the bread at the start of a meal. For most of the year, Jews eat leavened bread like this.

 At Passover, Jews eat unleavened bread, called *matzah*.

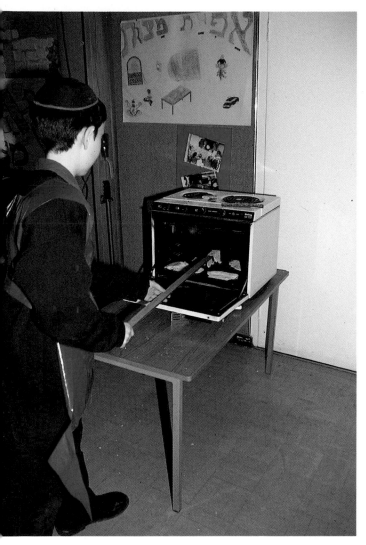

A schoolboy learns how to make matzah.

reminds Jews of the time long ago when the Jews left Egypt. They had to leave in a hurry, so they had no time to wait for their bread to rise.

FOOD IN THE FIRE

Not all Jewish families practice this ritual. But just before Passover begins, some children help their parents to burn any bits of leavened food, called chametz, that they have found in their search of the house. A small fire is lit outside the house, and the chametz is burned. The mother, father, or any adult says a prayer to God. In the prayer they say they have done their best to clear out anything that should not be in the house during Passover.

The family is now ready for Passover to begin.

Fire lit outside to burn the chametz.

13

 Reading at the Table

During the Passover meal, the story of the Exodus is told. The story is read from a special book called the Haggadah, which means "telling." It is written in Hebrew and English.

Everyone takes turns reading from the Haggadah.

TAKING TURNS TO READ

When everyone sits down for the Seder, each one has a book beside his or her plate. Even the children have their own Haggadah. This sometimes has pictures the children have colored in. People take turns reading a part of the Haggadah story found in the Book of Exodus in the Bible. (Even though Moses is not in the Haggadah, he is at the center of the story of the Exodus.)

Pharaoh, the Egyptian leader.

PHARAOH, THE SLAVE DRIVER

The story of the Exodus begins long ago in Egypt. Pharaoh, the Egyptian leader, was worried about the large number of Jewish people there. He decided to make them slaves so that they could not harm him. He made them work long and hard. As more and more Jews were born, he decided that Jewish boys had to die.

One day, a mother hid her baby boy in some

14

reeds so that the Egyptians could not kill him. The Pharaoh's daughter found him and took him to her palace, where he grew up safely. He was named Moses, which means "drawn out," because he was rescued from the river. As Moses grew up, he saw how cruel the Egyptians were to the Jewish people.

THE BURNING BUSH

One day, Moses was so angry with an Egyptian's cruelty that he hit him. The man died, so Moses had to escape. He left Egypt and worked as a shepherd in the deserts of Sinai. Then a strange thing happened. He saw a bush on fire, but the bush was not harmed. Moses went to have a closer look. It was then that God told Moses to go to Pharaoh and say to him, "Let my people go." So Moses went and told Pharaoh to free the slaves, but Pharaoh just laughed. So God sent plagues to punish the Egyptians. (To find out the rest of the story, look on the next page!)

Some copies of the Haggadah, like this old one, are very beautiful.

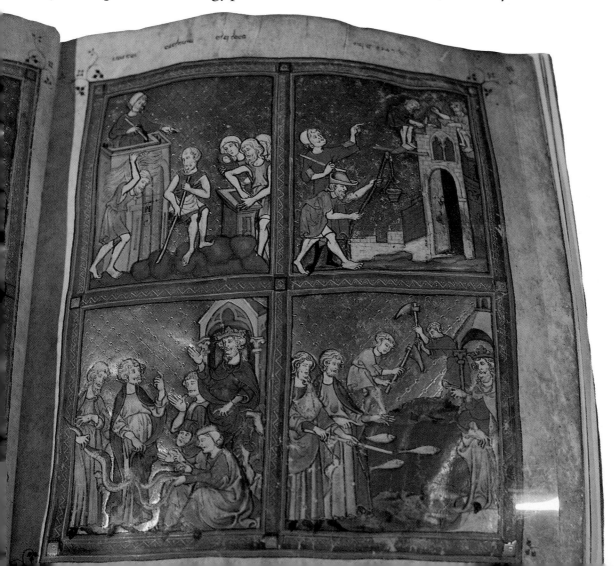

The Story of the Ten Plagues

When Pharaoh refused to set the slaves free, God made terrible things happen to punish the Egyptians. He sent ten different plagues that hurt the people, their animals, and their crops.

WHAT NEXT?

The first plague that God sent turned the waters of the Nile River red. The fish died, and the people could not drink the water, but Pharaoh would not let the Jews go.

The Nile River, in Egypt.

So God made frogs come out of the Nile and swarm over the land, but Pharaoh would not let the Jews go.

So God sent a plague of lice across the country, but Pharaoh would not let the Jews go.

Next, God sent wild animals across the land. Then God sent a disease that killed the cattle; then a plague of boils. But Pharaoh would not let the Jews go.

Huge hailstones dropped from the sky. Then a swarm of locusts ate the crops; and darkness came over the

The ten plagues in a modern Haggadah.

16

land for several days. Still Pharaoh would not let the Jews go.

The tenth plague was the most terrible. The first son in every Egyptian family died.

After this last plague, Pharaoh let the people go.

THE FIRST PASSOVER MEAL

Before he sent the last plague, God had told the Jews to cook a meal of roast lamb and to be ready to leave. They did not have time to make regular bread to take with them, so they made flat bread that did not rise.

While the Jewish people ate their meal, the angel of death passed over their houses. Only the Egyptian sons were killed. This is why the holiday is called Passover, because the angel passed over the houses of the Jews.

A page from a very old Haggadah that shows the first Passover meal of roast lamb.

 Setting the Table for Seder

The Seder reminds Jews of the story of how they were set free long ago. The table must be set in a special way.

A PLATE IN SIX PARTS

A Seder plate is divided into six parts, for the six special foods that will be eaten. Each food is a symbol. First, there is an egg that is hardboiled and slightly roasted. It is a reminder of spring, of new life, and of the temple in Jerusalem. Fresh herbs, usually parsley, are another reminder of spring, new life, and hope. Bitter herbs and horseradish remind the Jews of how bitter their slavery was. (Sometimes the bitter herbs include a type of bitter lettuce.) *Haroset* is a mixture of apples, nuts, wine, and spices. It is eaten to remind the Jews of the mortar, or clay, the slaves used when they were building. A shankbone, from a leg of lamb, reminds Jews of the temple where sacrifices were made to God and of the Passover lamb offering.

A Seder plate.

WATER AND WINE

What else is on the table? Salt water that the parsley is dipped in is there to remind Jews of the tears of the slaves in Egypt. Wine or grape juice is there, too. Even children have their own glass that is filled four times during the meal. In a separate dish there are three pieces of matzah, the unleavened bread, under a special cover. Candles are lit to show the light and joy of the festival, and seats can have cushions. Sitting in comfort reminds the Jews of their freedom. Last, but not least, everyone has a copy of the Haggadah beside their plate.

Children are part of the Seder.

The table is set for the Seder.

The Order of Events

Seder means "order." The Seder is eaten in a special order. There are fifteen parts to this Passover meal!

Children at school wash their hands during the Seder.

BLESSINGS

Jews always thank God before eating or drinking. Tonight, they start the meal by blessing the wine and drinking the first glass. During the meal, they drink three more glasses of wine. Twice during the meal, some Jews stop to wash their hands in running water. They eat foods like those on the Seder plate in a special order. At the end, they sing songs and pray together. The Seder includes a full, family meal. It will probably be the family's favorite foods, as long as they are kosher for Passover. The Seder starts soon after nightfall and lasts for several hours.

HIDE AND SEEK

Near the beginning of the meal, an adult hides a piece of matzah, which is called the *afikomen*. Later, the children go off to look for it. The meal cannot end until the *afikomen* has been found, so whoever finds it gets a prize!

WHERE'S ELIJAH?

Everyone eats a piece of the *afikomen* and drinks a glass of wine or grape juice. An extra glass is filled for the prophet Elijah, a Hebrew prophet.

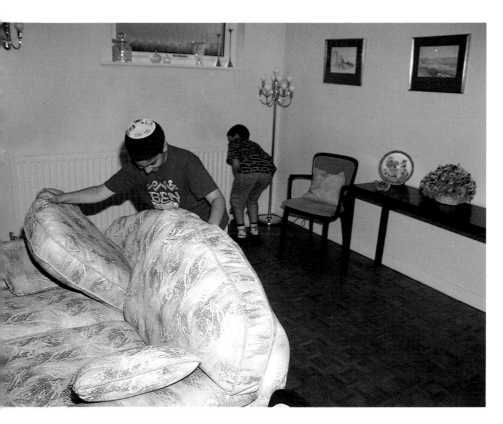

Searching high and low for the *afikomen*.

Found it!

Jews believe he will one day return to Earth. At Passover, children go to the door to see if he is on his way to their house.

QUESTIONS

The children in the family learn about Passover by asking four questions during the meal. They ask "Why do we eat only matzah? Why do we eat bitter herbs? Why do we dip parsley in salt water? Why do we eat bitter herbs or horseradish with haroset?" Can you find the answers in this book?

21

 # Psalms and Songs

Songs and music are an important part of Jewish life and worship. At Passover, everyone joins in the singing during the Seder and afterward, too!

SONGS IN THE SYNAGOGUE

Jews often use songs to "say" their prayers. They go to the synagogue to worship together. On special days, there may be dancing, and in some synagogues, live music is played on a variety of instruments. On some festival days, a traditional instrument is played. It is a shofar, made from a ram's horn and blown like a wind instrument.

Praying in the synagogue.

SEDER SONGS

Near the end of the Seder, most families sing some psalms from the Book of Psalms in the Bible. The psalms praise God and are thankful for God's goodness. At this point in the meal, the fourth and last glass of wine or juice is drunk.

People also like to sing traditional songs. One, called *Dayennu*, reminds Jews of all that God has done for them and helps them to count their blessings. After the meal, the singing may go on late into the night.

▲ Blowing a shofar.

Children and teachers enjoying singing together at their Seder at school.

23

🍇 The Passing of Passover 🍇

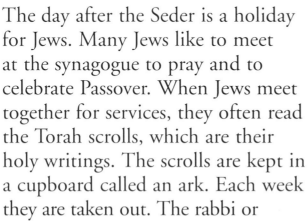

Does everything return to normal after the Seder? Not quite!

A MEETING PLACE

The day after the Seder is a holiday for Jews. Many Jews like to meet at the synagogue to pray and to celebrate Passover. When Jews meet together for services, they often read the Torah scrolls, which are their holy writings. The scrolls are kept in a cupboard called an ark. Each week they are taken out. The rabbi or cantor reads or chants part of the Torah. The next week he or she reads the next part aloud. It takes a year to read through to the end.

The synagogue is the place of worship for Jews. But it can be other things, too. It can be a school where

A synagogue in Russia, where old friends like to meet.

An 18th-century synagogue in France (left). Torah scrolls kept in a cupboard called an ark (above).

children and adults go to learn Hebrew and to learn about Judaism. It can also be a place for friendship, where people worship together and make friends. And it is a special place at holiday times, when Jews celebrate together.

BACK TO SCHOOL

Some people have a week's holiday at Passover and go out with their family. But most people go back to work, and children go back to school. For the rest of Passover, the main difference from the rest of the year is the food, which still must be unleavened, or specially prepared for Passover. And don't forget that, for some Jews, the cutlery and dishes are different, too. When Passover comes to an end, they are wrapped up and put away for another year.

25

"Next Year in Jerusalem"

Many Jews live in Israel, but many more live in other parts of the world. Passover is a special holiday, or festival, because it brings Jews together from many different countries.

PASSOVER PILGRIMS

Israel is quite a new country, but Jews have lived in that part of the world for at least 3,000 years. Today there are Jews on every continent of the world. They may speak different languages and wear different clothes, but, wherever they live, they have one thing in common. They all think of Jerusalem, in Israel, as the central place of their religion.

Passover is an old pilgrim festival. A pilgrim means "one who travels to

A Jewish family in Yemen (above) and visitors to Israel from Ethiopia (right).

26

holy places." In the past, Jewish pilgrims traveled from far and wide to celebrate the festival together in Jerusalem.

THE WESTERN WALL

Many years ago the Jews had a temple in Jerusalem where they worshiped God. The temple was destroyed by the Romans. All that remains is part of the outer wall.

It is called the Western Wall. Jews travel to Jerusalem at special times in their lives, and at festivals, such as Passover, to pray at the Western Wall.

Today, Jews all over the world say at Passover time, "Next year in Jerusalem." For some, that wish comes true.

Praying at the Western Wall.

Let's Celebrate!

Join in the fun! Try making this Seder plate and haroset. Use the pictures in this book to help you decorate the plate. Look on page 18 to find out about haroset.

MAKING A SEDER PLATE

You can make a colorful Seder plate as a decoration. If you want to eat from it, put a layer of plastic wrap over it first.

Materials:

- a paper plate
- paints, crayons, or felt-tipped pens
- colored cardboard or paper
- clear glue
- safe scissors

Directions:

1. Paint the plate in a pale color and let it dry.
2. Divide the plate into six sections with a pen.
3. Draw one of these shapes in each section, or cut them out and stick them down. Draw an egg, a bone, parsley or green herbs, bitter herbs, and haroset—a mixture of apple, nuts, cinnamon, honey, and grape juice. Use the pictures in this book to help you.
4. Now decorate the plate with leaf patterns, flowers, bunches of grapes, and olives.

MAKING HAROSET
Things you will need:
- four eating apples
- a cup of nuts
- a cup of raisins
- one level teaspoon of cinnamon
- four tablespoons of grape juice

Directions:
1. Peel and core the apples. Then chop or grate them finely.
2. Chop the nuts.
3. Mix all the ingredients together.

Glossary

Cantor A leader of prayer and music.
Chametz The last remaining pieces of leaven burned before Passover begins.
Haggadah The book used at Passover Seder. The word *Haggadah* means "telling."
Hag Sameach A Passover greeting meaning "Happy Holiday!" or "Have a joyous festival."
Hebrew The traditional language of Jewish scriptures and many Jews.
Jerusalem The ancient city of David and capital of Israel today.
Kosher Refers to foods allowed by Jewish dietary laws. It means "fit" or "proper."
Leaven Substance that causes dough to ferment and rise, for example, yeast.
Matzah Flat bread, like a cracker, used at Passover.
Pesach The Hebrew word for Passover. Festival celebrating the Exodus.
Seder Usually refers to the ceremonial meal in the home, eaten at Passover.
  The word *Seder* means "order."
Synagogue A building set aside for Jewish public prayer, study, and meeting.
Tradition A custom—a way of doing something passed down from parents.

Further Reading

Atlas, Susan. *Passover Passage.* Toral Aura, 1991.

Bogot, Howard I. and Rober J. Orkand. *A Children's Haggadah.* CCAR Press, 1994.

Fishman, Cathy. *On Passover.* Macmillan Children's Group, 1995.

Goldin, Barbara D. *The Passover Journey: A Seder Companion.* Viking Children's Books,
  1994.

Roekard, Karen. *The Santa Cruz Haggadah Kids Passover Fun Book.* Hineni Concisus,
  1994.

Schotter, Roni. *Passover Magic.* Little, Brown. Boston, 1995.

Schreiner, Elissa, and others. *Let's Celebrate Passover!* Astor Books, 1993.

Wylen, Stephen M. *The Book of the Jewish Year.* UAHC Press. New York, 1995.

Index